D1237812

All-American Fighting Forces

BUFFALO
SOLDIERS

JULIA GARSTECKI

BLACK
RABBIT
BOOKS

Bolt is published by Black Rabbit Books
P.O. Box 3263, Mankato, Minnesota, 56002.
www.blackrabbitbooks.com
Copyright © 2017 Black Rabbit Books

Design and Production by Michael Sellner
Photo Research by Rhonda Milbrett

Library of Congress Control Number: 2015954862

HC ISBN: 978-1-68072-000-6   PB ISBN: 978-1-68072-285-7

Printed in the United States at CG Book Printers,
North Mankato, Minnesota, 56003. PO #1794 4/16

Web addresses included in this book were working and appropriate
at the time of publication. The publisher is not responsible for broken
or changed links.

Image Credits
Alamy: North Wind Picture Archives, 4–5, 15, 18; arizona university:
31; Bridgeman Images: Buffalo Soldiers
in Pursuit (color litho)/Remington, Frederic
(1861–1909), 7; cowboyindianart.com: Les LeFevre,
26; Frederic Remington Art Museum: 22–23; Granger:
NYC, 12; http://soldiers.dodlive.mil: U.S. Army and Her-
itage Education Center, 28–29 (background), 32 ; Library
of Congress: 3, 17; Mansfield Library Montana: Archives
and Special Collections, 24; Nebraska State Historical
Society: image RG1517–PH000093000030_SFN103306,
Cover; National Park Service: 25; Shutterstock: Cattalli-
na, 9; Everett Historical, 11, 21; Joshya, 6, 28–29; US
Army: 27; Wikimedia: Back Cover, 1
Every effort has been made to contact copyright
holders for material reproduced in this book.
Any omissions will be rectified in subse-
quent printings if notice is given
to the publisher.

Contents

4

CHAPTER 1

To the Rescue!

About 50 soldiers hid behind their dead horses. Hundreds of American Indians surrounded them. The soldiers had been forcing them off their lands. The Indians were fighting back.

After seven days, the trapped soldiers were weak. Many were hurt. All of them were hungry. Then they heard loud hoof beats. The Buffalo Soldiers were coming to the rescue!

Fierce Fighters

The Buffalo Soldiers were **fierce** fighters. These African American soldiers helped settle the western United States. They protected **settlers** from angry American Indians. They also built roads, parks, and buildings.

The name Buffalo Soldier was a nickname. American Indians called the soldiers this name. Soon, everyone used it.

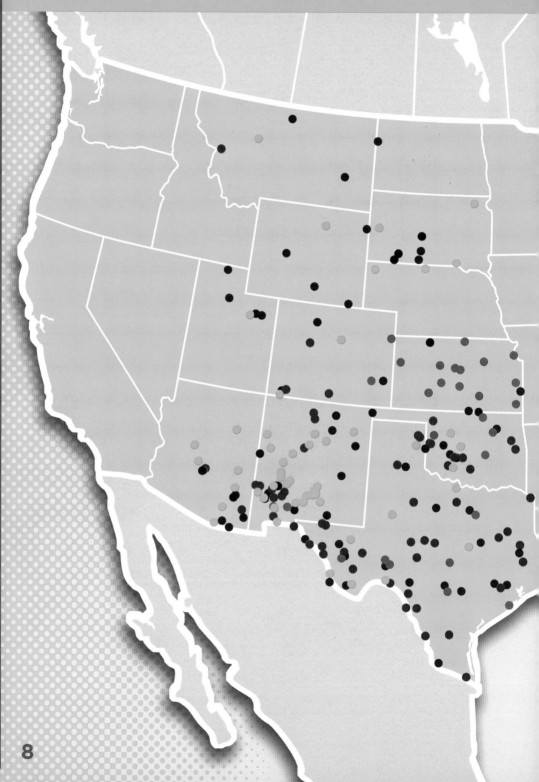

● 1860-1870
● 1870-1880
● 1880-1890
● 1890-1900
● Unknown

CHAPTER 2

A New Army

When **slavery** ended in 1865, many blacks didn't have jobs. In 1866, the United States created army units for African Americans. The army was a place where they could earn money. Soldiers were given places to sleep and food to eat. They also learned new skills.

11

BUFFALO SOLDIERS
BY THE NUMBERS

1 WOMAN
PRETENDED TO BE
A MAN TO JOIN

13
DOLLARS
EARNED
EACH
MONTH

ABOUT
5,000
BUFFALO
SOLDIERS PROTECTED
THE WESTERN UNITED
STATES.

Unfair Treatment

Many white people disliked African Americans. They didn't think blacks were as good as whites. The army put black soldiers in units by themselves. They couldn't train or fight with white soldiers.

White officers treated black soldiers poorly. The soldiers were given rusty guns and bad food. Whites were also **violent** toward blacks. Some white soldiers killed black soldiers.

ALL-BLACK UNITS
CREATED IN 1866

Moving Westward

In the late 1800s, thousands of Americans moved west. These settlers pushed American Indians off their lands. The Indians fought back.

Buffalo Soldiers were sent west to help. They quickly became known as tough troops. They also became known as hard workers.

CHAPTER 3

Fighting Battles

The battles with American Indians were deadly. Many Buffalo Soldiers and Indians died. The Indians lost these "Indian Wars." The government set aside land for American Indians. The Buffalo Soldiers forced tribes onto those **reservations**.

Protecting Settlers

The American Indians wanted their lands back. Sometimes, they sneaked away from the reservations. They attacked settlers. Buffalo Soldiers protected the settlers. They fought the Indians in more bloody battles.

The Buffalo Soldiers' saying was "We can! We will!"

Spanish-American War

The United States went to war with Spain in 1898. The battles were fought in **Cuba**. Buffalo Soldiers went there to fight. For the first time, Buffalo Soldiers joined white soldiers. They helped win the war. And they proved blacks could fight with whites.

Soldiers during the Spanish-American War

306,760 soldiers total

2,500–3,000 Buffalo Soldiers

BUFFALO SOLDIERS' WEAPONS AND GEAR

HAT

RIFLE

GLOVES

SADDLE

CARTRIDGE BELT

BOOTS

The soldiers also created many national parks. They built trails and put out wildfires. They caught thieves stealing timber. Buffalo Soldiers were the nation's first park rangers.

CHAPTER 4

Building a New Nation

Buffalo Soldiers helped build roads, parks, and towns. They explored the land and drew maps. They also put up **telegraph** wires.

Strong and Brave

Buffalo Soldiers worked from Minnesota to California. They fought many battles. They helped settlers. And they proved black soldiers were as brave as white soldiers.

Medal of
Honor

The Medal of Honor is the highest award for military service.

VALOR

3,497
total
recipients

1 woman
23 Buffalo
Soldiers

1867
American Indians call black soldiers "wild buffalo."

1866
U.S. government forms six all-black army units.

1865   1875   1885   1895

1880
Buffalo Soldiers fight with outlaws from Mexico.

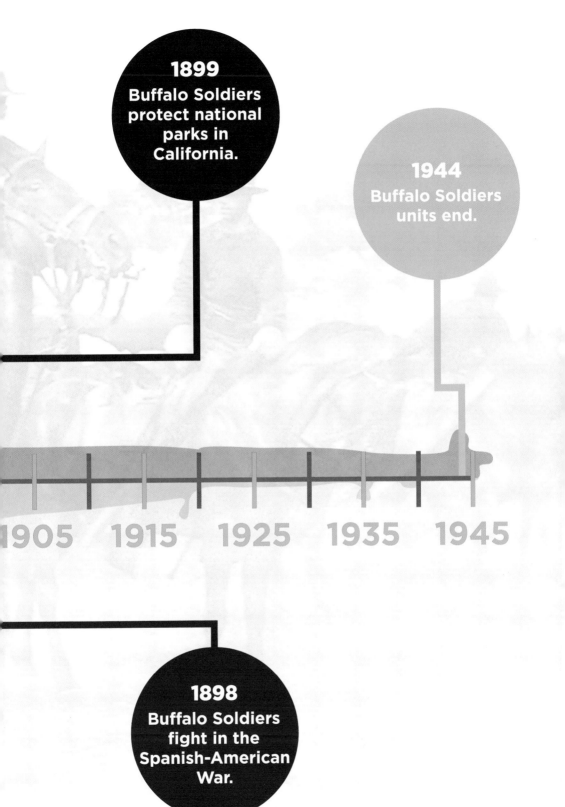

1899
Buffalo Soldiers protect national parks in California.

1944
Buffalo Soldiers units end.

1905   1915   1925   1935   1945

1898
Buffalo Soldiers fight in the Spanish-American War.

Cuba (KYU-buh)—an island in the Caribbean Sea

fierce (FEERS)—strong or intense

reservation (re-zur-VAY-shun)—an area of land that the U.S. government kept separate as a place for American Indians to live

settler (SET-luhr)—a person who goes to live in a new place where there are few or no people

slavery (SLAY-vree)—the practice of owning slaves; a slave is someone who is owned by another person and forced to do work without pay.

telegraph (TEL-uh-graf)—an old system of sending messages over long distances by using wires and electrical signals

timber (TIM-bur)—trees that are used for wood

violent (VI-oh-luhnt)—using physical force to cause harm to someone or something

BOOKS

Honders, Christine. *Buffalo Soldiers.* Heroes of Black History. New York: Gareth Stevens Publishing, 2015.

McHugh, Erin. *National Parks: A Kid's Guide to America's Parks, Monuments, and Landmarks.* New York: Black Dog & Leventhal Publishers, 2012.

Mills, Cliff. *The Buffalo Soldiers.* Fact or Fiction? Hockessin, DE: Mitchell Lane Publishers, 2015.

WEBSITES

The Buffalo Soldiers
www.nps.gov/prsf/learn/historyculture/buffalo-soldiers.htm

Buffalo Soldiers
www.nps.gov/yose/learn/historyculture/buffalo-soldiers.htm

Buffalo Soldiers: The Unknown Army
www.youtube.com/watch?v=QLGvTqFPHCw

INDEX